POINTS OF TRAUMA
A CONSIDERATION OF THE INFLUENCE PERSONAL AND COLLECTIVE TRAUMA HAS ON CONTEMPORARY ART

This book is dedicated to the memory of the artists I have known who have laced their work with the fabric of their own lives and who are no longer here to inspire us.

For Konstanty, Hugo and Sebastian

An artist's history should become stains that seep through from the bottom of the paper, and are embedded permanently within the work, but are not dark enough to stop you from translating the text in your own way.

INTRODUCTION

In his essay '*Forgetting Things*', Sigmund Freud discusses how a person's mind will block locations, people, and events that are linked to, but not necessarily directly associated with, traumatic experiences. For instance, you may block out the location of a shop because someone you have fallen out with lives nearby. An artist's work can act in a similar fashion. The creation of a work can replicate the function of the mind by compartmentalising trauma but, instead of locking it away to be forgotten, it chews it up into pieces and presents it as a new entity: something released from the individual.

There is a vast history of artists who have drawn from personal or collective trauma. Frida Kahlo's relationship with her body, Vincent Van Gogh's view of his own personality, Eugene Delacroix's confrontation of the class uprising within the French Revolution come to mind. Most of the artists who have utilised this access have presented bodies of work that a viewer can instantly connect with. There are very few nuances within the meaning of the final piece. It can be described as overt. However there are others who have hidden trauma within their practice. One is the Dutch artist Bas Jan Ader who produced a series of works that dealt with his father's death at the hands of the Nazi's in World War Two as well as confronting his religious upbringing. But without knowing his back story, the connection is barely visible.

My own practice has always been formed from a confrontation with trauma. In 2008 I undertook a project to film people reading a poem by Rupert Brooke that had stuck with me since I first encoun-tered it during my Mother's treatment for breast cancer when I was a teenager. In 2010 I took part in a scripted wrestling match that reflected on an incident where I had been attacked by a gang of teenagers in a London park, and my first feature film script was based largely around the feelings associated with the suicide of a relative.

At the age of thirty I went to university for the first time to study a Masters in Fine Art at Central St Martins and it was here that I began to analyse the presentation of these events and their im-portance in my work. The bones of this essay are drawn from thoughts in a piece of writing I started at this time but have since wound their way through a much larger exploration. The original text raised a question that has since grown in perspective largely due to world events over the past five years, but also due to new personal experiences. I wanted to know where the line between repre-senting my own trauma was drawn in a way that could be engaging to a viewer and where it was just an act of catharsis. This in itself stimulated an unexpected outcome. I began to resent my work and my process for being self indulgent. As I uncovered the nature of the work by artists such as Francis Alys and Doris Salcedo, I found my presentations irrelevant. I never wanted to use art as a form of therapy but I did see the power of art to change, to inform, to assist, and to influence others. My work did none this.

A second outcome began to emerge. The investigation into the practice of others in itself became a work of art. I stopped seeing it as a text that could educate the reader in the practice of other artists and instead saw it as a journey I had to take, one that would assist in applying context to my exist-ence in a world that has dramatically changed through technology, communication, and politics in the past twenty years. With this in mind, I structured the text into parts, using my previous practice of catharsis as interludes that sit between and lead into chapters that explore the nature of numerous artists' work.

Each of the five sections in this book addresses different aspects of trauma: Loss and Therapy, Revelations, Violence, Failure, and Validity. As the investigation unfolded, I found myself wandering through obvious examples of personal and collective events into more nuanced areas. These places shed a light on the use and abuse of collective traumas within society and politics to influence public view points. As such, there are points where I found myself looking outside of the art world for both influence and interpretation. From the use of imagery in Barack Obama's presidential campaign to the simplicity employed by Donald Trump to connect with an abandoned class who had grown tired of elaborate artistry, through to Doris Salcedo's representation of everyday living under the spectre of Civil War in Columbia.

LOSS AND THERAPY

Goodbye Baa

Baa crept into the dining room where my camp bed was crammed in between the table and his old record player. He knew I would still be awake. Putting his finger to his lips he encouraged me to whisper. He then proceeded to recite a familiar story, an exaggerated description of his days in the RAF during World War II. He told of a daring rescue involving a Spitfire pilot who had been shot over one hundred times but still managed to fly back to his home shore. I listened intently, too young to question the elaborate details. Once the story finished, he took a sip of his whisky, and reached for the large headphones attached to the record player. Smiling, he placed them on my head. The ritual ended in the same way it always did. Elton John's Crocodile Rock sang me to sleep.

The impact of the front door hitting the wall woke me. The headphones had long since slipped off, and I was entangled in the cord. As always the entrance to the dining room had been left slightly ajar, and I could just make out a fluorescent yellow jacket rush past. The room itself flickered with blue light. Then the stretcher followed. Baa's face was covered with a plastic mask. My mother cried from a far away room. Probably the kitchen. Then a hand pulled the dining room door closed.

I knew what had happened, even if I did know the details. No one came to open the door after the light stopped flashing. I stayed where I was. It wasn't until the next morning that I was informed that the stories of wartime heroics would not be told to me again.

Doris Salcedo, Briony Campbell and Louise Bourgeois.

In her 1997 installation Unland, Doris Salcedo presents a series of three fragile tables, a continuation of her focus on domestic items brought together in order to confront loss and mourning. In this case the confrontation is the ongoing Civil War in her home nation of Colombia. Her research led Salcedo into and through the lives of those had been left behind: lovers, families, and close friends - all who had witnessed a homegrown war claim the lives of many through battles with drug lords, terrorists, and even their own nation's soldiers. Estimates put the loss of life since the conflict began in the mid 1960's at over two hundred thousand, with a further five hundred thousand displaced from their homes. The charity UNICEF says that, of those affected between 1958 and 2013, one in every three have been children. The initiation of the conflict can be traced back to the United States' backing of the Colombian governments anti-communism actions in the late 50's and 60's. Although if traced even further back, roots began to appear during the 1948 occurrence of _La Violencia_, a separate conflict that resulted in the assassination of political leader Jorge Eliécer Gaitán during 1948. A peace deal was finally signed between the Colombian Government and the FARC rebels on the 26th August 2016. In positioning herself within close proximity of those whose lives had been directly affected, Salcedo sought to highlight the everyday nature of war when fought over many years for the same pieces of land.

In _Unland_, she utilises the fragility of materials to portray the testimonies of the victims. Salcedo uses silk and human hair woven into the tables' woodwork or engulfing the object itself to encourage the viewer to a point of contemplation that allows the lives hidden in the work to emerge. This silence is key. She has verbalised numerous times that just as with heroes, the victims of violence are driven to silence as the world around them becomes estranged. It's this thought that we can all relate to. The minutes, hours, days and months after we suffer loss can seem overtly quiet in retrospect. Personally I cannot recall a single conversation or word spoken during similar times and my memory only selects the gestures: (A colon is better) the holding of a religious artifact in search of a channel to the lost, the touching of a stone that guards someone's remains in a vain hope that disappearing skin may feel a single stroke, the extension of a hand to another who is suffering. These are the things I remember.

Salcedo revisits the situation in Columbia throughout her work. In the commissioned installation *Shibboleth* she churned up the concrete floor at the Tate Modern in London and created a crack that ran the length of its Turbine Hall, fluctuating in depth and diameter as it consciously and directly confronted the immigration policy of Europe. In explaining the work, Salcedo said in the exhibition's guide that it supposedly stands outside catastrophe but, when you look inside, you get the feeling of catastrophe. In a video published on YouTube to promote the installation she talks about the conflict she has personally suffered as a holder of a third world passport, and defines herself as someone who has always seen this from the other perspective, the perspective of the defeated people, not the perspective of triumph. Going further, she describes the presence of the immigrant directly affecting the culture of Europe and the experiences suffered by those with similar heritage whilst crossing borders as extreme versions of racial hatred. In 2016 the points she raises have come to the fore within European culture. With the mass arrival of refugees from the Middle East and Africa, the rise of far right beliefs re-emerged. Not since the 1920's had popular thought been impregnated by the seeds of anti-immigration on the continent that had defeated fascism in 1945. Many comparisons have been drawn to rhetoric used by politicians and the press in 2015, 2016 and 2017 to that of propaganda used by the far-right nearly one hundred years before, and these associations are indeed present. The British newspaper, the Daily Mail, is the obvious marker with headlines in 1938 describing *German Jews* pouring into the UK, and in 2016 describing Syrian mi-grants as a *swarm*. I find it ironic that I have not visited many Jewish households in North London where the paper is not read every morning for breakfast, but its history seems to have been long since forgotten.

Salcedo's untitled installation at the Istanbul Biennale of 2003 saw her fill the space between two buildings with a mountain of wooden chairs, perfectly flush with book end like walls on either side. She described this as a *topography of war*, and in her choice of material she again highlights the effects of war on everyday life, chair after chair representing the previously owned land in which victims sat. As the ground is stained and trampled, you still have to get your milk. You still have to work. Life doesn't stop. It carries on just with added danger. Although the installation gives us a vision of the singular event, or even racial genocide, Salcedo has been keen to stress that she was just addressing personal experience. An interesting point is also raised during another filmed interview with Salcedo for the San Francisco Museum of Modern Art.

She discusses the lack of museums and galleries with great collections the people in third world countries have access to. This leads her to explain that not being able to see art work in its physical form drives you to images in books. These two dimensional representations, accompanied by explanatory texts, in turn cause artists such as Salcedo to lean heavily towards the theoretical. Perhaps this in itself explains why there is so much potential for thought both overtly and between the lines within her work.

Where Salcedo dealt with loss through violence, the photographer Briony Campbell attempted to use her camera to say goodbye to her father. Her work *The Dad Project* begins after he was diagnosed with a terminal illness, Campbell documents the ensuing months via her lens and, with this method comes an insightful, heart wrenching window into someone preparing herself for loss. The project begins with a very simple shot of a building engulfed by the rays of the setting sun. The im-age is no different to a thousand others taken by people all over the world at the very same second, aside from its location and Campbell's understanding of her tools. The handwritten caption that sits alongside simply reads, *'the sunlight supported me this year'*. It is at this moment Campbell delicately takes our hand and invites us to walk with her for a little while.

The first few images continue to allude to the situation through the captions. A milk bottle is accompanied by the phrase *'at first it seemed to confirm my own optimism he'd get better'*. Then a mid shot of Campbell lying in bed is accompanied with - *'after the terminal diagnosis, it served to comfort my mourning'*. Still she talks of the sun's light, a phenomenon usually associated with healing powers. In Campbell's case, the power to heal her grief.

Only after six photos does the first image of her father appear, a close up shot of his shoulder, and the remnants of medical tape that had been used to attach what appears to be a drip. It is here that we are confronted with the reality of the situation. I recall sitting in front of someone who had been recently hospitalised. My focus was drawn away from background noise, facial expressions and even the larger situation as a whole. It was drawn only to the spoon sitting in mashed peas, tilted up in the food tray that sat on the bed in front of him. The minor detail seemed both a distraction and the sum of the events playing out in front of me. I see this exact feeling within Campbell's image. This image is accompanied by a story of her father's tears when his wife departed the ward before his requested dedication to her was played on on the hospital's radio station. A selection of photographs follow that depict his solace in the garden of her home, and again the light becomes key. The images are bathed in gold and long shadows are cast by the sun. They seen almost refreshing, as does the image of her father propped up in a hospital bed, his face emblazoned with a genuine smile that only someone who has been suffering can possibly create. It is the smile of a man who wholeheartedly adores the personal connection of the moment he is being captured in. A man who realises his future and recognises his past.

The story continues through his gradual deterioration in health, and again Campbell punctuates this with a shot of the sun breaking through the leaves of a tree, this time captioned - *'today we knew he would die soon. I went outside I looked up at the sky. It was perfectly beautiful'*. Her comparison of nature's effects in driving forward with light and creation against its harsh reality makes this project more than just a personal journey, or indeed a therapy.

Campbell's series can be seen merely as dealing with impending loss. Its stark ending is a shot of a yellow skinned, lifeless hand laid across her own. She writes simply - *'me and dad'*. However, interwoven between the harsh reality it portrays and the bright sunlight that acts as a guide, Camp-bell tells us of singing and laughter. The many levels of this work create a hard to critique effect. In fact by writing about it I have begun to feel a high level of guilt, but then I remember that Campbell has put this into the world and not locked the images into an album that resides only in her own personal space. She has, as Salcedo would say, found a way to keep the memory of her father alive, as well as to overcome her own grief.

Louise Bourgeois often discussed the notion of art as therapy, a fact she never ran from it in her constant addressing of a tumultuous relationship with her own father and her mother's death when she was only eight years old. Brought up in a middle class family living on the rim of Paris, her father's affair with her governess would be the nail in own their relationship's coffin. She once recalled how her father created a model of her from a tangerine skin and made disparaging remarks as a phallus emerged from inside. A number of years later she would pose with a phallus of her own making for the photographer Robert Maplethorpe, whilst wearing a bright fur coat. Her success as an artist came late in life, following the death of her own husband, the American art historian Robert Goldwater. She was seventy when she stopped being a figure on the periphery of the New York art scene and became acclaimed. It was at this point that Bourgeois would release the story of her father to the world.

Bourgeois often stated that to be an artist was a guarantee to your fellow humans that life's harsh reality would not make you a murderer. Her statement echoes an underlying truth that art can channel the emotions of its makers and offer them some form of release from captivity.

REVELATIONS

Brothers and Sisters

I knew I had a sister, but I didn't know where she was. It wasn't until I was 17 that I chanced upon a girl who said she knew her. It took a few months for me to pluck up the courage to make something happen, and when I did I was still very sceptical.

After a few months, I told my father. She wanted to meet. She wanted to know why he hadn't been in her life for 10 years. I remember many years before sitting with my father in his car. On the back seat was a sack of Christmas presents. Tears were in his eyes. He was shaking. A taxi driver walked over to us and, like an illicit drug deal, my father passed the sack from our car to his. He greased his palm with a ten pound note. I don't remember if any words were said.

When eventually they did meet years later, there were more tears. In that moment I saw the man my father used to be, and the man he had become.

Joseph Bueys, Anthony Gormley, Louise Bourgeois and Tracey Emin

Perhaps one of the greatest falsities of the 20th century art world was the story created by Joseph Beuys. He had been listed in the German Air Force during World War II and as a Luftwaffe pilot he had flown numerous missions over the course of three years. His plane had also been shot down. However Beuys had told of being rescued from a snowy fuselage by Tartars who had taken him to a tent and nursed him back to health by covering his body in fat and wrapping him in felt. In fact there were no Tartars, or fat, or felt, merely a German military hospital. He also spoke of how his epiphany had occurred on waking up inside the Tartar's tent and having a new drive, one that would inspire his artistic output, a story that would make box office gold for Hollywood, probably a fact Beuys himself contemplated. His career growth mirrored the rise of the Silver Screen.

When the discovery of Beuys' manipulation of the truth became known in the 1980s, the world did not cry foul as they would for a politician. Instead, no one really cared. By this time, and for many decades already, the eyes and ears of the public had been exposed to explosions, plane crashes, and hand-to-hand combat retold with great elaboration by the studios under the hills of Los Angeles. The story is also being claimed as the source for one of Beuys' most recognisable works, The Pack, a VW minivan with its rear doors bursting open as an army of 24 wooden sleighs each equipped with felt blankets, fat, belts and torches spill out. *Does it matter that the truth was stretched in the justification of the work?*

Although referring to literature, the overlying theme of Roland Barthes' text *Death of the Author*, can easily be placed into the realms of art. Once the work has left an artist's studio, is there really a necessity to carry with it the back story of the artist's life in order for it to successfully communicate? There are obvious contemporary examples where this is not the case.

As a sculptor, Anthony Gormley's work does not require us to know that he was born to a wealthy German father and an Irish mother in

Yorkshire England. In fact, this makes no difference to the perception of his work, nor indeed is there anything of any interest in these facts. However the tabloid culture of the 21st Century has driven the world into a desire for every last detail of a person's life. Maybe if Gormley had an affair with a footballer's wife, his *Angel of the North* would take on another meaning? We could decipher it as an ageing man opening his arms to the young WAG's of Gateshead, inviting them into his land.

Anish Kapoor was born to a Jewish mother who had emigrated from Baghdad and a Punjabi father who was in the Indian Navy. Kapoor himself studied in the UK where he now works. These facts, and any further details are completely unnecessary in the reading of Kapoor's work. Had he become a political figure spearheading a movement against the U.K.'s coalition government of 2011, these facts would take on new meaning and in turn affect the reading of his work. The mirror placed by the side of the Serpentine in Hyde Park, London could be read as a reflection of British attitudes towards immigration, reminding those who look into it that the land is already populated by many colours and creeds and that the sky is an opening to the rest of the world. At this point the argument begins to arouse interest. When the public's desire for back story and gossip is coupled with the artist's desire to create we find an area in which stories are told regardless of intent. There are many working artists who shy away from the need to layer their work with their own life. The Polish filmmaker Krzysztof Keislowski said that his life and its influences should always be present in his work but that the viewer should never be able to notice it.

These perceptions of Kapoor and Gormley may play with humour and politics, but they also highlight an increasingly obvious fact. Since the growth of the Hollywood press in the 1950s, a niche in society has developed that is purely consumed by the lives of others. This niche has grown to become a need of the public as a whole and has begun to seep into and stain other industries. There is a hunger for stories of love rats, traumatic family emergencies, and judgement errors surrounding those who been given the pedestal of celebrity or have been elected to a position of responsibility. Over time, this hunger has become a need. To some extent the importance of individuals' private lives overshadows their ability to do the job they are employed to do. It is true to say that these people know they are in a position where they must keep their house in order, but should they expect to be hounded as they are?

This question is not the important one. In fact the real question is, do they want to be hounded? It is fair to say that some probably do, and that they have even built careers from allowing stories of personal trauma to make it to the press. Possibly it is not just an allowance, but sometimes a feeding. It is this feeding of stories to gain publicity and arouse the public's interest that parallels certain artists' use of the life's trauma as a backbone of their practice. As I previously mentioned, Louise Bourgeois did not reveal her history until her husband's death, whereupon she gained a level of notoriety that revolved around her life story. Her critical appreciation began when the viewer was told what to think.

Similarly Tracy Emin has always confronted her personal history directly in the eye through her practice. In one of her early works, *Everyone I Have Ever Slept With*, the names of her lovers between 1963 and 1995 were sewn into the fabric of the tent. Emin's story was there in the title, the work, and even the exhibition guide. Little has changed throughout her career, and the documentation of miscarriages, provincial sea side town lives, sex, and even self loathing has become an important visual reference to social and cultural issues within the late 20th and early 21st century. Her collaboration with Bourgeois again highlights Emin's desire of the story. Presented with a number of sketches by the American, she has told of her inability to add her touch and complete the project before Bourgeois died in 2009. Having taken the work all over the world with her, eventually the day came that she felt comfortable to commit to paper, but why did it take her so long? Was it her admiration and respect for Bourgeois? If so, this is laced with irony. Bourgeois' late rise to fame, first in America and then internationally, mirrored the rise of Emin during the 1990s. It was at a similar time that their works both became acknowledged in the history of contemporary art regardless of the difference in ages. The personal emotions she may hold do not necessarily match the art world's perspective in which the two arrived in the public consciousness almost simultaneously.

In one specific piece that forms part of the collaboration with Bourgeois, the torso of a pregnant woman is depicted. The pink flesh gives way to an X-ray inside the stomach depicting a black and blue blob. Almost like an ink stain. With this mark, I am gratefully and willingly lost with the collaboration's contributor. Is it Bourgeois, a woman who had two of her own children as well as her adopted son Michel? Or was it Emin, who after two abortions discovered she was unable to have children of her own? I want to not know who drew this mark. I want this question to remain open. If my mind is drawn to a specific conclusion about the depiction of the growing child I lose something within the image. I lose my ability to frame it within my own existence. I am a man. I could never bear a child. In some ways this is a deeply unsettling fact; in others it is vastly reassuring. The pain of childbirth and the constant fluctuation of the body throughout life seem to me to be the greatest sacrifice that women have to bear. I cannot ever imagine it. However the bond created by being able to nurture an embryo into life and subsequently see what has grown within you for the first time is something that fills me with jealousy.

I have lost a child during pregnancy. It is heartbreaking, and something that allows me to understand people bury their grief behind the birth of future children or increased work loads. The constantly spoken lines of *'it wasn't meant to be'*, or *'there will be plenty of opportunities in the future'* are obviously meant as olive branches by those who speak them. But the underlying feeling is failure. Not the failure of finishing a painting you think is you best work that then doesn't sell, or writing a book that vastly misses the point you were trying to make. It's the kind of failure that rips at the human inside you. It leaves your ego untouched. Instead it aims for the very instinct you were born with. As a man, this feeling pales in comparison to the emotions a woman goes through during this time. With this feeling in mind, I want to look at that blue mark on the painting and not know its future. I want to distance myself from Emin's pain as well as my own, but also I want my pain to be represented in the work and, as such, I don't want to feel the pressure of Bourgeois' ability to bear children making me feel useless. Emin's obvious contribution to the image is the text underneath that reads 'dark, black, lonely space.' This does exactly what it says on the tin. It tells me her per-spective without interfering with the stomach, the incubation. In my reading of this work I purposely block what I know about each of the artists in order to keep this question open. If I allow myself to analyse brush strokes or technique, or even look at the series as a whole, then I lose the connection I have. I therefore lie to myself.

In discussing not becoming a mother, Emin has stated that she sees her paintings as her children, and describes the feeling of failure that engulfed her as being soothed by seeing her work exhibited. In contrast, Bourgeois hated to exhibit. Jerry Gorovoy was Bourgeois' chief assistant for nearly 30 years and the person who in some form was responsible for her rise to fame. While she was content to make, he pushed her to exhibit. She stopped going to her own exhibitions, becoming only interested in her current creation and built up a hatred of losing Gorovoy during the installation process. Frequently she would remind him that the need to exhibit was his.

By telling you who they are and why they became, do the artists open doors for further interpretation, or do they close them? With Beuys, I remember seeing *The Pack* on two or three occasions before I knew of the tale he had created to endorse his work. Its imagery was striking, conjuring thoughts of red ants carrying sandwich crumbs back to their home from a discarded picnic basket, or even a Swiss Army training camp. Knowing what I know now about Beuys, and looking at the work with a singular perspective, it drives me to a specific story, one created in the artist's head, one I enjoy, but not quite as much as the freedom of my own imagination. This can, of course, work as a positive. If an artist can drive a viewer to a specific thought pattern, then there is a greater chance of success in achieving transferences of an exact attitude.

VIOLENCE

An Attack

It was 1.30am and I was returning home from work. The night bus crossed the River Thames and the city of London lay illuminated in front of me. In the five years since I arrived here from a childhood in the British countryside, the view had not lost its appeal. As the vehicle navigated the Old Kent Road, I watched lights flicker on chicken shops, groups of people outside night clubs, and those like myself who were navigating their way back to their own beds.

It was a clear sky. If I got off the bus a stop early I could cut through Friendly Gardens and smoke a cigarette looking over the view of Canary Wharf to the north. I could be lost in my thoughts for a little while longer.

The idea seemed like a good one but, after drifting away for a while, I became aware of a figure. A teenage boy. He came closer and asked me for a smoke. I only had roll ups. I took them from my pocket and offered him the chance. Before he took them from my hand something hit the back of my head. I fell.

I awoke nearly naked. My jeans around my knees. One boot off. My torso completely exposed. My right hand fell to my ribs and found them sticky. A gash in my side bled. I was wearing contact lenses and one had left its place in my eye. My vision was blurred. A voice spoke in a language I didn't recognise and then I felt myself lifted. Nearly on my feet, I saw three maybe four figures. They asked me where my wallet was. I hadn't taken it to work. They didn't care. Blows rained down. To my chest, my face. I fell again. Feet connected with my nose and my eye sockets. I bled more.

They had my keys. They asked where I lived. My girlfriend was home. They couldn't know. I had to get out of this and I fought. I was on my feet and running. I took the wrong route out the park on purpose. As I entered the street I started shouting, maybe even screaming. I banged doors, and people soon came out their houses. Looking behind me I could see no one was following. I stopped and rested, my hands on my knees, taking a shortcut to get home. My ribs were broken, my shoulder dislocated and my vision full of blood.

When my girlfriend answered the door, awoken from a restful sleep, her face told me what had happened. In the bathroom I looked in the mirror and eventually collapsed.

From Image to Stereotype
the subject as hero and efforts to counter that.

1985.

An infant, maybe three years old, stands up. He is emaciated and has been lying naked on the floor. His siblings, covered in thin blankets, huddle around each other. He weakly pushes himself to his feet. We see adults sitting nearby, hundreds of them sprawling across a desert waste land. The child appears to search for something, then uses his arms to support himself as he attempts to crawl a short distance. He has no energy from the lack of food.

The film was accompanied by a piece of popular music in which a man sings, *'Who's going to drive you home, whose going to pay attention when you scream'*. It showed victims of a famine that had engulfed the people of Ethiopia in a way that no incident of such enormity had been presented via the mass media before. In doing so it was possibly the first example of the immediacy we now ex-perience with social media and the transference of news.

The film became the cornerstone of an event called Live Aid that would see musicians around the world come together to perform in order to raise funds and awareness for those affected. It was before the rise of artists into mass public consciousness in the early 90s, but is now replicated by charity auctions of artworks for every heart breaking event that occurs. Half way through the concert, the video is introduced by David Bowie and a silence descends on Wembley Stadium in London. For four minutes the silence continues as harrowing images continue to play. The camera pans across the faces of a crowd draped in collective sadness. As the footage draws to a close, we see the shape of another young child; it is wrapped in hessian. Its face is covered as its mother places its lifeless body onto the ground. The music fades and, for a few seconds, the silence continues. Then the crowd cheers.

Why do the crowd feel the need to applaud at this point? Have they been overtaken by the emotion of the images they have just seen? Do they feel like their presence at this event has drawn an end to the children's suffering? Are they just impressed by the quality of the film? Or maybe they are excited that another musician has arrived onto the stage? There is no denying the fact that the event itself provided much needed exposure and support to those who were close to dying, something that can't and shouldn't be detracted from, but somewhere here there is a deeper reaction. At the time this video had played, it had already been seen in varying forms around the world as part of news broadcasts. People were familiar with it. As humans we naturally build resistance to that which affects us, and as such when presented with the same images we do not invoke the same initial emotions. However, once these images are paired with music a new set of feelings begin to overtake us. A euphoria. This presentation succeeded in doing just that, and once again reminded people that they were at a concert with every famous face in the world present, a once in a lifetime experience that would be retold for generations. It had deeper meaning and, by attending or watch-ing, you had become part of that meaning, part of a solution.

The problem is that the video and the event combined to do something else. They started the numbing of a generation. Overtime, people built up a resistance to similar images to the point that there is currently a large section of society that feel they are hounded into supporting worthy caus-es. They stereotype a plea for help as 'liberal', as if there is a negative connotation for balance in the world. In 2016 images of refugees escaping the war in Syria were used by far right political campaigners across Europe, in particular during the Brexit campaign in the UK where backgrounds to advertisements described migrants as a swarm or even a plague. One particular image depicted the politician Nigel Farage smugly standing in front of a poster showing an arcing wave of thousands of refugees attempting to find a new home. The slogan *Breaking Point* accompanied it in large red letters. Underneath, a smaller text talked of taking back control. It begged the question of what taking back control over a situation like this means. It is certainly not sovereignty or tighter borders. It can only draw a line to further violence, a reality that day by day has slowly materialised. The migrants are fleeing a war that has largely been influenced by Western interference in the region. This interference has not been drawn to a conclusion, one that would stabilise the lives of the population. Instead, marred by waging wars under false pretences, such as the second invasion of Iraq, Western Allies removed their presence and allowed private corporations to provide both security and assistance in rebuilding. This profiteering from the tragic loss of life in turn led to further fragmented reactions and conflicts.

In the space of thirty years, a large part of the population of the western world had gone full circle. No longer did startling images stir the need to help. Instead they aroused the need to protect their own. For a short time the mood swung when the image of Alan Kurdi, a three year old Syrian child who had drowned crossing the Mediterranean sea and whose lifeless body had washed up on a Greek beach, appeared in the worldwide press. However Kurdi's death soon became perceived as a symptom of terrorism in Europe rather than a result of the war in his former homeland. There are, of course, many other factors to investigate, but there is an obvious connection to the way in which the media and artists have used images to intentionally pull the heart strings of the public in a drive to make them help. We live in a time where many have found themselves in an abandoned class. Those who worked at every level in industrial organisations, from shop floor to middle management, have been forgotten by the governments that closed their industries down and, as a result, when they find themselves being asked to open their doors to others, they look inside themselves and think, *there is nothing left for them to have.* Therefore they want to close the door.

These people have been subjected to an art world that has emboldened the individual's pain. For a large part of the last fifty years there have been very few household name artists who have presented the pain of anybody but themselves. In the early 19th Century Eugene Delacroix painted *Liberty Leading the People*, a call to action for the French. The image of a strong female figure holding aloft the Tricolor flag whilst standing, almost floating, above the bodies of the fallen, depicted the pain and hope of an entire nation simultaneously. The late 20th and early 21st Centuries have given us very little art of social value. In fact, when art has contained political motive, it has been barely tolerated or simply demeaned. In itself this act has given the mass public a valid reason to despise art that serves as a therapeutic process for the artist or, even worse, seeks to drive them to assist a cause.

Throughout the 1990's, documentary photographer Sebastian Salgado captured images of children affected by war. From the genocide in Rwanda to Kurds in Northern Iraq. The collected stills provide a glimpse at what humanity is capable of. When the context of time is applied, we can see a series of conflicts occurring almost simultaneously across the world, displacing families and orphaning children. A generation will grow up knowing that those before them allowed the murder of their parents. They let their siblings be starved and their grandparents be beaten and raped. The West is currently happy to consider itself a civilised society as much as it is happy to look away from the problems its needs and desires have caused around the rest of the world.

In 2007, Steve McQueen presented *Queen and Country* a large wooden cabinet that contained 155 sheets of postage stamps on which were placed the faces of men and women killed in Iraq. McQueen himself then led a campaign for the stamps to be presented by the Royal Mail, a task that ultimately failed with the British institution afraid to offend families of the dead even though they stated their support for the tribute. This could have been an artwork that crossed boundaries from the gallery system into the public consciousness, but the fear of a public body to present both personal and national loss blocked the transference of the work.

In 2008, I undertook a project to document the work of the poet Rupert Brooke through filmed read-ings of his poetry by over two hundred individuals. During the course of the work I also began to investigate Brooke's life. One of the trips I took was to the village of Dymock in Gloucestershire where he had resided prior to the First World War. It was here that he would meet Robert Frost and Wilfred Wilson Gibson, amongst others, and form the Dymock Poets. In the village I met with an elderly lady called Barbara Davis. In a shed at the bottom of her garden she had spent many years collating an archive that covered all the poets' lives and works. Over a cup of tea and a slice of cake we talked about their importance, and she raised a very interesting point. The British press had waged a propaganda war at home during the war. It portrayed the soldiers as victorious in every battle, rarely letting on that there had been any loss of life. The words written by the war poets gave the British public the brutal truth. Their heavy verses describing freezing trenches and the bodies of fallen soldiers told people of the reality that faced those on the front lines. They painted a picture that prepared families across the country for the loss of fathers, brothers, and sons, whilst a governed press protected them from their worst fears.

Also in 2007, the Tate Britain commissioned Mark Wallinger's installation *State Britain*, a recreation of peace campaigner Brian Haw's protest in Parliament Square, London. Adorned with signs protesting the same war McQueen's work confronted. The work also stayed firmly put in the gallery system. In fact, all it really achieved was to remove the actual from the world and place it into a fabricated entity. In this environment it could speak to no one other than the converted. Any British viewer who would enter the Tate gallery would probably be familiar with the original setting and have his or her own sympathies and beliefs prior to this presentation. Any one not from the island would also be familiar with the protest due to the nature of the signs on display. It would do nothing but commentate the fact that protest in Britain was becoming futile, and even outlawed. Of course this in itself is a valid point to raise but, can an installation of this nature, presented in an establishment where the average visitors are unlikely to break away from their middle class values and use their Saturday off to march, really do anything? You could argue that some of those important enough to guide the country's laws may be in attendance and may start to reconsider their stance. However, in truth, it has been a long time since a work of art, film, or a piece of music had the resonance to really change the minds of those at the top of political life.

The ethics of punk in the 1970's certainly did a great deal to place the hidden emotions of Britain's youth into the mainstream. They used photocopied fanzines, brash slogans on t-shirts, and large scale public interventions such as the infamous boat trip along the Thames by the Sex Pistols to infiltrate an established media and, subsequently, the Governments status quo. However, those in control learnt a great deal from the movement and over time have acted to placate a similar rising of rebellion. Could there indeed be an argument that the proposal of opening of museums for free by the Labour Government in the late 1990's was a way to retain some form of control over the work that could or couldn't be displayed within the walls? By giving the public a gift they were, in fact, hiding the new found control over the system. Of course the institutions were public prior to this, but once the income of the institution is dependent on Government funding, does it not become part of the state?

To mirror the rise in the Government backing of institutions in the UK, the Arts Council's expansion in 1994 and rise in funds due to the flow of income from the National Lottery provided a new resource for the funding of individual artists and projects. There can be no doubt in the benefit to society as a whole in providing income to artists. However, this can also be seen as a form of control. An artist working for the State cannot produce work that truly questions the State. There will of course be works such as McQueen's or Wallinger's that sit gently on the border but, in truth, they never cross into territory that allows the viewers to really consider their own position in the system. It is, if you like, a commentary on a perspective, mostly dealing with recent history, never questioning future actions.

FAILURE

Entrepreneur

For two years I had tried to build a business.

I had never really been financially inclined and my mind was led by creative impulse. So it should come as no surprise that a year later, in the space of 48 hours, everything had gone.

A break-in with no insurance at the office, an event with no sponsorship or financial backing was run with blind faith. Both contributed to the end.

Tacita Dean and Bas Jan Ader

As part of the series entitled *Disappearance At Sea*, Tacita Dean focused on failed attempts at crossing large bodies of water. Notably, she discussed the journey undertaken by Dutch artist Bas Jan Ader. His crossing was part of a trilogy. The first stage would see him walk across Los Angeles, the second sail the Atlantic, and in the final he would arrive in his former home of Amsterdam. The journey was never completed. His boat was found 150 miles from the coast of Ireland, battered and unmanned.

Dean discussed Ader's challenge in an essay published to coincide with the opening of the *Disappearance At Sea* exhibition. In this she points out that his only small challenge to himself outside of the journey being an artwork, was to break a record by completing the trip in the smallest vessel ever to have done so. However, Dean's work began its focus with a journey by Donald Crowhurst. As with Ader, Crowhurst's journey was unsuccessful and, although he was never found, his boat was. Interestingly the basis of his disappearance stemmed from two incidents. The first was the fabrication of charts and timings during a race across the sea; the second was his study of Einstein's theory of relativity whilst riding the waves. This study led him to investigate his own theory, and it was the discovery of a final equation that drew him to the conclusion that he had achieved the impossible and solved the mystery of the universe. This revelation was so powerful that it is claimed he threw himself into the water and drowned. However, the knowledge of his previous deception in fabricating the charts leads us to question the validity of this story.

It was a copy of the book detailing Crowhurst's story in the faculty locker owned by Ader that threw doubt onto his own ending. Did he plan to make us believe that he disappeared and, if so, is this his work of art? These questions were again raised over 30 years after Ader vanished because of the prominence of the canoe man story that broke in 2007. John Darwin was a businessman in the UK whose finances had taken a turn for the worse in 2002. He subsequently staged his own disappearance by leaving a broken canoe and numerous personal effects on a beach. The insurance company paid a large sum to his wife who emigrated to Panama. However she did not go alone. A photograph appeared on the Internet five years later showing her and John enjoying a new life abroad. An everyday man had managed to achieve a task set out in spy films, and the public were captivated by his story.

Ader's history as an artist is short. There are only seven works that can be truly attributed to him. Whilst studying in Amsterdam he reportedly use the same sheet of paper on which to draw for an entire course, constantly rubbing away the image until the paper bore more in eraser marks than lead. The bulk of his video work was supposedly recorded over just one weekend. His *Fall* series depicted him entering unnatural journeys to the ground, leaving gravity in control of his outcome. Probably the most notable, *Fall 1*, sees Ader sitting in a chair on top of the roof of a house. He leans the chair and it eventually succumbs to nature's force, toppling with Ader down the first pitch, over the veranda, and into the bushes below. In another, he cycles towards the bank of the river, oblivious to the obvious. Then his bicycle, with him on board, meets the edge, they tilt down and break the surface of the water, disappearing from sight.

It is the moment he lets go when Ader loses control of the direction of the work. He takes the power of the artist and places it in the hands of something else. Some would say god, and it could be speculated that Ader himself was a deeply religious man. He grew up in a church with a preacher for a father and it is a certainty that God was in his life as a child. He did not advertise his faith as an adult, but did his father's influence still remain?

So are Ader's *Fall* works possibly an investigation into his faith? Does a man who sits on his own roof and purposefully begins to tumble have to believe that something will save him? Or can we easily conclude that a fall from the one-storey Veranda will result in little more than a broken arm if you're unlucky?

Ader's father was a preacher during the Second World War in Holland. He was arrested by the Nazis and imprisoned before being taken to a woodland where he was executed for sheltering Jews. Years later Bas Jan would take a series of photographs of himself falling over in a wood, an act that could well have been a re-enactment of his father's death. Following the execution, the Germans gave Ader's mother 15 minutes to collect her belongings and leave the house. She ran through each room throwing clothes and other items out the windows to the ground below. Again, many years later Ader would photograph his own house in Los Angeles with the roof covered in clothes.

Before the war Bas Jan's father also did something that would pave the way for his son's final adventure. One day he walked into the kitchen and said to his wife '*I am going to Palestine*'. His wife chuckled and replied by asking how he would get there. His reply was "by bicycle". Sure enough, he began his journey across Europe and arrived in Jerusalem on his bicycle. His had not been a journey of adventure as his son's would be in 1971, but instead it was a search for the miraculous. His mother would bring him and his brother up hoping they would follow in his father's footsteps. Bas Jan did not, at least not immediately. Instead he travelled to America where he would continue studying art, ending up in Los Angeles. After time his study would turn into teaching. He became disillusioned by the role he now had come to play. He had married, got a good job, and did not want for things; however he was laden with an artistic guilt that said he wasn't trying hard enough to be what he wanted.

If we knew none of this, we would not speculate that his beautiful film *I'm Too Sad to Tell You* was in fact Ader taking on the role of a weeping Jesus who was burdened with the sins of man. The tears and contortions of Ader's face are human and evocative enough to strike us all on many levels without having to scratch away at moments from the artist's history in order to find meaning. Maybe he was trying to represent a tearful Christ. His journey into the sea could also be symbolic of Christ's solitude in the desert, where for forty days and forty nights he would begin to understand the task ahead of him. Perhaps Bas Jan Ader just wanted to understand his task. Perhaps by doing so he needed to understand the history of those who went before him, hence the discovery of Donald Crowhurst's biography. But then we have the title he gave his final fling. *Searching For The Miraculous*

VALIDITY

Education

It was not an easy decision to return to education at the age of thirty. I had not studied since my mother's treatment for cancer had interrupted my exams at the age of 18, and I left school with no real qualifications.

I cannot blame anyone but myself.

When you choose to pause your responsibilities in life for twelve months at a later age, some things become increasingly obvious.

Up until this point I had undertaken a largely relational practice, asking others to contribute their words to my work. I thought it more important to portray their emotions than mine in order to con-nect. Yet, as a backbone to each project I used my own back story. My own struggles. As if I was afraid to confront myself directly. As if my own identity was easier to find in the words of others.

Maybe I just didn't want to feel like I had been alone. Maybe I just wanted validity.

Francis Alys, Shepard Fairy, Jeremy Deller and Wolfgang Tillmans

Francis Alys rarely takes his work to a level of completion. Instead he holds it back in the hope that he can revisit or even replicate the work at a later date. In *A Story of Deception,* Alys initially trav-elled to Patagonia in order to film a bird that could only be found after days of endless walking. Once he assessed the footage he realised that he had, in essence, just made a nature documentary and became frustrated with it. However he also discovered a repetition within the work that he had not noticed first hand. The dusty desert roads threw up sand and heat to create mirages. It was these that would now become the focus. Alys' subject was found accidentally, but only because he allowed it to be.

In 1986, Alys relocated to South America after studying architecture in Europe. It was in Mexico City that he began to practise as a visual artist. His work *When Faith Moves Mountains* saw him recruit four hundred students in Peru who were each given a shovel and asked to walk in a line across a sand dune slowly displacing the ground. Finally the dune would be moved geographically by a few inches. The location was alongside one of Lima's many shantytowns that survive without running water or electricity, a community that has relied on word of mouth to create stories that have both entertained and become ingrained as a common history. The artist's intention was to create a new folk lore. His previous work had also relied heavily on creating rumour. However this particular event was filmed in its entirety and is now commonly presented in this form. The question that arises is that, if the work was truly about creating a myth that would be passed on through the stories of the students involved and the local witnesses, then is there a necessity to record the actions using the medium of film? The viewer does indeed see four hundred Peruvian students shoveling sand, mostly out of sync and with the result of nothing more than a few feet of dust above their heads, but would the story itself, as a tale of mythological values, not have generated a greater response to Alys' original goal? Is this not an example of an evocative artist feeling he needs to create something that can fulfill the capitalist notion of product? Or is this film an anthropological document?

If you look at Shepard Fairy's now iconic *Hope* poster, you will see an example of how an artwork can manipulate a public's political view point and at the same time document a specific moment in time, assisting in the development of a legend that is told through corridors, streets, and office blocks. Fairy initially printed three hundred posters with the word *Progress* accompanying a stylised portrait (independently of the campaign office) of Barack Obama. However, the viral success of the image soon inspired Obama's team to request the phrase Hope, and later Change as replacements. This combination of language and image ended up inspiring the American people and, although it is hard to quantify how much it influenced voters, it did replicate the iconic imagery that was familiar with other idolised leaders such as Che Guevara. This instant comparison by a viewer put Obama into the realm of a man fighting for people's freedom.

In contrast, the simplicity of Donald Trump's 2016 Presidential campaign slogan, *Make America Great Again* on a simple red baseball cap, removed the idolisation of the individual, something a number of Americans associated with Obama, and placed the emphasis back on nationalism. The slogan, with its minimal design merit, communicated to a different group of people, a people who were left behind by politics and globalisation and wanted things condensed into facts, true or not.

When British Prime Minister Theresa May called a snap election in early 2017, stating that unity in Parliament was necessary to deliver Britain's exit from the European Union, she used the phrase 'strong and stable' within the Conservative Party manifesto. A few weeks after the campaign had begun, posters appeared across England that read 'Strong And Stable My Arse'. These utilised the same simple design approach that Trump had used in his campaign. It was subsequently revealed that the posters had been created by artist Jeremy Deller who stated they were self explanatory. Deller has a history of political art and is one of the few artists who rose to fame in the 1990's to successfully use his work as a way to stimulate debate. In 2001 he produced The Battle Of Orgreave, a full reenactment of the clash between police and picketing coal miners that took place in 1984, under the veil of Margaret Thatcher's privatisation of the industry. A documentary film of the event was produced by Mike Figgis in which the left wing politician Tony Benn describes the way in which the BBC manipulated the footage to insinuate that the miners had been the ones to instigate the violence. Part of Deller's desire to recreate the event was in order to put straight the facts and allow history to be told in its actual truth, not the way in which the press had years on. Similarly in 2016, to commemorate the 100th anniversary of the Battle of the Somme, men dressed as soldiers, marching in unison appeared in public spaces across the UK. Onlookers at London's Waterloo station watched as actors stood in silence representing actual individual soldiers who had lost their lives in the battle. Deller succeeded in bringing both individual and collective trauma from one hundred years earlier into the mindset of ordinary people going about their everyday routines.

Also in 2016, as part of the commemoration of the 350th anniversary of the Great Fire of London, artist Martin Firrell was commissioned to make Fires Modern. The projections on the side of the National Theatre on London's Southbank directly confronted stories of progress within civil rights movements: The suicide of footballer Justin Fashanu, a moment that stirred the debate of homo-phobia in football, the force feeding of Mary Jane Clarke in Holloway prison as she protested for the right of women to vote in the UK in 1910, the words of the MP Jo Cox, who was murdered during the Brexit campaign of 2016 by a right wing terrorist. Fires Modern finds many forgotten stories in the history of progressive movements and asks the public to think on them. Presented outside of the gallery system, it achieved its aim. It asked the viewers to contemplate their own place in the history of their personal battles alongside the places of those who may have paved the way for them.

Wolfgang Tillmans' immersive installation at the Tate Modern as part of his 2017 retrospective fea-tured aspects similar to a nightclub. A number of projected screens displayed extracts of his video work, whilst a constructed soundtrack played and white spotlights rotated across the bare concrete. This created a unique feeling. Occasionally blinded by light, or overpowered by music, your eyes and ears remain active, searching the darkness for the next movement, waiting for a video to begin and wondering which screen it may appear on. Your neck stretches as you survey the wall behind you, quickly turning back as a screen appears on the opposite side. Something plays and you are transfixed. In between the films, in the time you wait and as your eyes adjust to the light, you search the actions of others. There are those who come in, and then quickly leave, deterred by the darkness or the loud dance music. There is a group of teenage students sitting cross legged on the floor, initially joking with each other before coming under Tillmans' spell, possibly having their first true encounter with an artist. Then there is the elderly couple who are wondering how art stopped being painting or sculpture in their lifetimes, but who simultaneously tap their feet to techno music. Those who stay for more than five minutes seem to enter into a challenge, one where they must outlast other people they have never met before, and will never meet again. As you leave the space, there is a connection to those who have lasted the same distance as you, and a mutual glance of humour aimed at those who did not allow themselves to fall into the experience. You wonder which anxiety or fear stopped them from becoming immersed, and even what the initial cause of that feeling was.

Tillmans creates a space where we are drawn into a natural instinct of voyeurism, a characteristic of his work as a whole. The people within the space and their actions are as much a part of the work as the videos or lights, but how does it differ in mainstream 21st Century culture? There is no doubting that people watching has been a sport engrained in human nature for eons. The interest of another person's nuances, the ability to judge without consequences, and the attraction of the stranger have drawn us all into thought long before Big Brother existed. Has the evolution of televi-sion just found a way to allow people to do this from the comfort of their armchair instead of braving the cold terrace of a cafe?

Or is there something more? Whilst there are obvious examples of artists who have been influenced by trauma, the true interest lies in the reading by the audience, the viewers who bring their divorce, their miscarriages, their wars and their sacrifices to the space in which art is presented. We cry when certain musical notes are paired with emotive words, or even when they are played alone. We get angry watching soap operas where families betray each other. We are overwhelmed by a sculpture that towers over our heads.

Howard Zinn stated that art which has a mass appeal as entertainment is necessary to make people feel good, even comparing it to a kind of religion or, as Marx labeled it, *opium for the people*. It is at this point that the eye must cast back to the late 1990's and the inception of reality television. Of course talent shows had existed long before, almost as early as the inception of the medium. However when cameras were trained on ordinary people for sustained periods, sometimes 24 hours a day, a new entertainment was born - one that lets the viewer think, 'thankfully I am not that stupid/fat/prejudiced' or, 'I wish I was that intelligent/funny/ talented'. These may well be thoughts that have previously existed within constructed drama; in fact you can trace it all the way to Shake-speare, and probably long before. The difference, however, is that you are now looking at a real person, someone you can judge and then take that judgement out onto the streets around you, applying it to others who act or dress in similar ways. The result is an immediate stereotype, one that allows you to feel safe in your own world. The true danger in this situation is that these shows are heavily manipulated through scripting, editing, and casting, along with many other contrived elements. Therefore the end product can nurture an individual's opinions into the stigmatisation of large sections of society, based only on the presentation of one point of view. Have we spent the last twenty years looking at the world in the way television executives have chosen to present it? After all, an everyday supermarket trip is of no interest. Yet when a task is devised that can separate people and enliven their fears in order for them to win essential food or toiletries, an element of tension is produced. How much has the influence of this use of constructed reality transferred into people's day to day existence?

There are days when we all just need to watch Tom Cruise race fighter jets over canyons, stand in front of a pickled shark, or hear Elton John sing about Marilyn Monroe flickering like a *Candle In The Wind*. There are days when we all need to be a little Hollywood. Similarly there are days when we wish to watch our peers in provocative and stressful situations and think *I'm glad that isn't me*. Some find religion an escape from traumatic experience, others find popular culture an escape from the trauma of everyday life.

There is no end to this discussion, as long as trauma exists we will continue to both hide it or exploit it, be it through forgetfulness or in our art.

A CONCLUSION OF SORTS

Freud continued on to say in his essay that painful memories are easily hidden for good reasons. It seems to me that there is an obvious similarity within the practice of certain artists to bury their own personal traumas within the work they create. Where the conversation dilutes is the point at which an artist confronts trauma on a collective scale. Doris Salcedo obviously has personal connections and experiences of the Columbian Civil War. However her work focuses on the effects on society as a whole. It is not her just own life she is hiding within her work; it is the lives of many thousands, an entire population. At this point we have to ask if it is possible for a singular voice to truly repre-sent such a large collection? It goes without saying that the search for an everyday existence within the environment is common, however the definition of that everyday existence is not.

As you will have noticed, this essay has strayed away from the confines of artist's practices and touched lightly on political movements. In the time in which it was written there was really no way this could not have happened. Everyone has become hyper aware of the divide that has grown around the world, with some countries leaning towards the right, some to the left, and some like France, forming a newly defined centre ground. What has become more than apparent in these times is the bubble people have built around themselves - both the influencers and the influenced. Groups have formed where only one dynamic is acceptable, and all seem to be focused on a particular change. The regulation of immigration, or the reverse. The return of state funded services or privatisation. The necessity of military defence, or peaceful action as a viable alternative. The regulation of corporations that conduct business on a worldwide scale, or the freedom to operate as a capitalistic entity. The world has changed rapidly through technological advancements and political thought has yet to keep up the pace.

With passionate artists returning to force their agendas and moving away from work of sellable value, society and thought can only be enhanced. However, the majority currently fall into an ecosystem that has been funded by individuals with beliefs on the opposing side. Artists have needed corporate collectors or state funding to continue to exist, and this is something that will never change. The question is: in that environment how does someone produce work that truly envelops the traumas society suffers as a whole and represent them in a way that is not regulated by their necessity to eat as a basic human?

Within the next fifty years society and individual needs will once again undergo substantial change. Now more than ever it is vital for artists to absorb the atmosphere that surrounds them, to chew it up, and then carefully conceal its implications within the thread of their work in such a way as to raise public consciousness.

Writing this text has allowed me the space to explore my own direction of travel. I have, as I previously mentioned, either relied on the words of others to express my view, or presented a brash unconvincing translation of my own experiences. This is no longer good enough. As people sit along the shores of beaches in makeshift camps waiting for the world to grant them humanity, it is not good enough to wallow in oneself. When people are killed in a fire because councils wish to save money and make an area look nicer instead of installing safety measures, it is not good enough to only talk about what has hurt you. In a world where military action is still the preferred choice of solving conflict, it is not good enough to only present your beliefs. These statements do not devalue the work of artists who trade in representations of beauty or form. It is in fact in these works that we sometimes find answers. I have seen many silent tears and much contemplation in front of Rothko paintings. Sitting before one of his canvasses for many hours could indeed be the mental journey that an individual needs to take in order to make a choice that will evoke a change within humanity as a whole.

The beauty, and indeed the danger, of any creative outlet is that judgement of the finished article is a matter of opinion. What one person takes from it can be entirely different from another. Just as Northrup Frye described the concealment of the New Testament in the Old, and the revealing of the Old Testament in the New, an artist's job is to conceal the trauma in such a way that it is revealed to the viewer.

THANK YOU

Linda Theodorou
Anne Lacheiner-Kuhn
Orly Nurany
Gareth Cadwallader & Christopher Ward for the many conversations that have led to this essay.
Sohrab Bayat, Jwan Yosef, Gala Knorr, Beth Fox, Edward Collinson, Pallas Citreon, Tom Mason and all from Charing Cross Road 2011 for continuing those conversations.
Alex Landrum Jnr, James Payton, Soline Pillet, John Schofield and all who have resided in Studio Bella.
Denise, Steve and Averill
Martin and Moon
Tom Williams
Paul O'Kane, Sally O'Reilly and Alex Landrum
Gabby Young and Stephen Ellis

1st Edition July 2017
Ruysdael Press
www.ruysdaelpress.com